Olivia Westwood

Standard Podcasting Guide

Your Comprehensive Guide to Launching, Growing, and Monetizing a Successful Podcast

First published by Olivia Westwood 2024

Copyright © 2024 by Olivia Westwood

All rights reserved. No part of this publication may be reproduced, stored or transmitted in any form or by any means, electronic, mechanical, photocopying, recording, scanning, or otherwise without written permission from the publisher. It is illegal to copy this book, post it to a website, or distribute it by any other means without permission.

First edition

This book was professionally typeset on Reedsy
Find out more at reedsy.com

Dedication

To the storytellers, the dreamers, and the curious minds who seek to share their voices with the world.

This book is for you.

Yours Truly,
Olivia Westwood

Epigraph

"Podcasting is storytelling for the digital age, a tapestry woven with voices that inform, inspire, and entertain."
Olivia   Westwood

Contents

Foreword 1
Preface 4
Acknowledgement 8
1. Introduction to Podcasting 11
2. Planning Your Podcast 15
3. Essential Podcasting Equipment 20
4. Setting Up Your Recording Space 26
5. Recording Your Podcast 31
6. Editing Your Podcast 36
7. Publishing and Distributing Your Podcast 42
8. Marketing and Growing Your Podcast 49
9. Monetizing Your Podcast 56
10. Measuring Success and Continuous Improvement 64
11. Legal and Ethical Considerations 72
12. Case Studies and Success Stories 79
    1.
    2.
    3.
    4.
    5.
    6.

7.
8.
9.
10.
11.
12.
13.
14.

Foreword

Foreword

Podcasting has become one of the most powerful mediums for sharing stories, ideas, and knowledge. Its rise from a niche hobby to a mainstream platform has been nothing short of meteoric, democratizing the airwaves and giving voices to individuals and communities that might have otherwise gone unheard. As someone deeply immersed in the world of audio storytelling, I've witnessed firsthand the incredible impact a well-crafted podcast can have.

The "Standard Podcasting Guide" is an invaluable resource for anyone looking to dive into podcasting, whether you're an aspiring creator or an established podcaster seeking to hone your craft. This guide meticulously covers every aspect of podcasting, from the initial spark of an idea to the intricacies of production and the nuances of audience engagement.

What sets this guide apart is its holistic approach. It doesn't just focus on the technical aspects of podcasting but also delves into the creative and strategic elements that make a podcast successful. You'll find comprehensive advice on defining your podcast's vision, developing compelling content, choosing the right equipment, mastering the art of editing, and effectively promoting your show. Moreover, it addresses the critical legal and ethical considerations that every podcaster must navigate.

One of the most valuable sections of this guide is the case studies of successful podcasts. By examining the journeys of popular shows like "Serial," "The Joe Rogan Experience," and "How I Built This," you gain insights into what works and why. These real-world examples provide practical lessons and inspiration, illustrating how diverse approaches can lead to success in the podcasting arena.

In addition to its thorough coverage of current best practices, this guide also looks ahead to the future of podcasting. It explores emerging trends and technological advancements, ensuring that readers are not only equipped to launch and grow a podcast today but are also prepared to adapt and thrive in the evolving landscape of tomorrow.

Podcasting is a medium of infinite possibilities. It allows for deep, meaningful connections between hosts and listeners, fosters communities, and can even spark change. Whether you're passionate about storytelling, education, entertainment, or advocacy, podcasting offers a platform to amplify your voice and reach a global audience.

As you turn the pages of the "Standard Podcasting Guide," you'll find yourself equipped with the knowledge, tools, and inspiration needed to embark on or enhance your podcasting journey. Embrace the insights offered here, and remember that every great podcast begins with a single idea and the courage to share it with the world.

Happy podcasting!

[Olivia Westwood]

Preface

Preface

Welcome to the "Standard Podcasting Guide," your comprehensive resource for mastering the art and science of podcasting. Whether you're a seasoned broadcaster looking to refine your skills, an aspiring podcaster just getting started, or a business professional seeking to leverage podcasts as a powerful marketing tool, this guide is designed to provide you with the insights, strategies, and inspiration you need to succeed in the dynamic world of podcasting.

Podcasting has emerged as one of the most influential and accessible mediums for storytelling, education, and entertainment. With millions of podcasts available and billions of episodes downloaded worldwide, the podcasting landscape is rich with opportunities for creators to share their voices, connect with audiences, and build thriving communities. But with this vast potential comes the challenge of standing out in a crowded market, maintaining high-quality content, and continually engaging your audience.

This guide is structured to walk you through every stage of the podcasting journey. From conceptualizing and planning your show to producing and distributing episodes, and from marketing and monetizing your podcast to measuring success and evolving with industry trends, each chapter delves into critical aspects of podcasting with practical advice, real-world examples, and actionable strategies.

You'll learn how to:

Define Your Vision: Identify your niche, target audience, and unique value proposition to create a podcast that resonates.

Develop Compelling Content: Master the art of storytelling, scripting, and interviewing to produce engaging episodes.

Equip Your Studio: Choose the right equipment and software to ensure professional-quality recordings.

Produce and Edit: Navigate the technical aspects of recording, editing, and mastering your episodes.

Distribute and Promote: Leverage platforms, SEO, and social media to reach and grow your audience.

Monetize Your Podcast: Explore diverse revenue streams and create sustainable income models.

Analyze and Improve: Use metrics and feedback to refine your content and strategy for continuous growth.

Navigate Legal and Ethical Considerations: Understand the legal landscape and uphold ethical standards to protect your podcast and reputation.

Learn from Success Stories: Gain insights from successful podcasters and apply their strategies to your own journey.

Prepare for the Future: Stay ahead of emerging trends and technological advancements shaping the future of podcasting.

Throughout this guide, we emphasize the importance of authenticity, creativity, and persistence. Podcasting is not just about the technology and techniques; it's about connecting with people, sharing meaningful stories, and making a lasting impact. Whether you're interviewing fascinating guests, sharing your personal insights, or exploring niche topics, your voice has the power to inform, inspire, and entertain.

As you embark on this podcasting adventure, remember that every successful podcaster started with a simple idea and a passion to share. With the right tools, knowledge, and dedication, you too can create a podcast that captivates listeners and stands the test of time.

Welcome to the "Standard Podcasting Guide." Let's get started.

Yours Sincerely,
    Olivia   Westwood

Acknowledgement

Acknowledgements

Creating a comprehensive guide like the "Standard Podcasting Guide" requires the support, insights, and encouragement of many individuals and organizations. I am deeply grateful to everyone who contributed their expertise, experiences, and time to make this book possible.

First and foremost, I would like to thank the countless podcasters who generously shared their journeys, challenges, and successes. Your stories not only inspire but also provide invaluable lessons for aspiring and established podcasters alike. A special thanks to those who permitted us to feature their podcasts as case studies. Your willingness to open up about your processes and strategies has enriched this guide immensely.

To the podcasting community at large, thank you for fostering a spirit of collaboration and innovation. The forums, social media groups, and meetups where podcasters gather to share tips and advice have been a constant source of inspiration and practical knowledge.

I am profoundly grateful to the industry experts and mentors who provided insights into the technical, legal, and creative aspects of podcasting. Your contributions have ensured that this guide is not only comprehensive but also accurate and relevant to the ever-evolving podcasting landscape.

A heartfelt thank you to the beta readers and reviewers who took the time to read early drafts and provide constructive feedback. Your input was instrumental in refining the content and ensuring that it meets the needs of our diverse audience.

Special thanks to my editorial team, whose hard work and dedication were crucial in bringing this guide to fruition. Your meticulous attention to detail, creative input, and unwavering support have been invaluable.

To the designers and production team, thank you for your talent and effort in creating a visually appealing and user-friendly guide. Your work ensures that readers have a seamless and enjoyable experience.

I also want to acknowledge the various podcasting platforms and tools that have empowered countless creators to bring their voices to the world. Your innovations continue to push the boundaries of what is possible in the podcasting medium.

Lastly, to my family and friends, your patience, encouragement, and belief in this project have been a source of strength and motivation. Your unwavering support has made this journey not only possible but also profoundly rewarding.

Thank you all for your contributions to the "Standard Podcasting Guide." This book is a testament to the collaborative spirit and passion that drive the podcasting community. May it serve as a valuable resource and inspiration for all who seek to share their voices through the art of podcasting.

[Olivia   Westwood]

1

Introduction to Podcasting

Introduction to Podcasting

What is a Podcast?

A podcast is a digital audio or video file series that listeners can stream or download from the internet. Podcasts typically focus on a particular theme or topic, such as true crime, comedy, education, or technology. Episodes can range from a few minutes to several hours and are usually released on a regular schedule, such as weekly or biweekly. Unlike traditional radio, podcasts offer on-demand content, allowing listeners to consume episodes at their convenience.

History and Evolution of Podcasting

Podcasting has its roots in the early 2000s, emerging alongside the growing popularity of MP3 players and the development of RSS (Really Simple Syndication) feeds. The term "podcast" was coined in 2004 by journalist Ben Hammersley in a Guardian article, blending "iPod" (Apple's popular portable media player) and "broadcast." Early pioneers like Adam Curry and Dave Winer helped popularize the medium by creating tools and platforms for podcast distribution.

Key milestones in podcasting history include:

2005: Apple added podcasts to iTunes, making it easier for users to discover and subscribe to shows.

2009: The release of the "Serial" podcast, which significantly boosted mainstream awareness of podcasting.

2014-2015: A surge in podcast popularity, with more people listening and more creators entering the space.

The Growth of Podcasting and Its Impact

Podcasting has grown rapidly, with millions of podcasts available across various platforms. This growth can be attributed to several factors:

Accessibility: Podcasting is accessible to both creators and listeners. Creating a podcast requires minimal equipment and technical knowledge, while listeners can easily find and consume content on their smartphones, computers, or other devices.

Variety: Podcasts cover an incredibly diverse range of topics, appealing to niche audiences and providing content that might not be available through traditional media.

Intimacy: Podcasts often create a sense of connection between hosts and listeners, fostering loyal and engaged communities.

The impact of podcasting is significant:

Media Landscape: Podcasting has disrupted traditional media, offering an alternative platform for storytelling, journalism, and entertainment.

Education and Awareness: Podcasts have become valuable tools for education and raising awareness on various issues, providing in-depth analysis and perspectives.

Monetization and Business: Podcasting has opened new revenue streams for creators through sponsorships, advertising, listener donations, and premium content.

In summary, podcasting has evolved from a niche hobby to a mainstream medium, transforming how people consume content and offering opportunities for creators to reach global audiences.

2

Planning Your Podcast

Planning Your Podcast

Defining Your Niche and Audience

Before launching a podcast, it's essential to identify your niche and target audience. Your niche is a specific area or topic that your podcast will focus on. To define your niche:

1. Passion and Expertise: Choose a topic you are passionate about and knowledgeable in. This ensures you can create engaging and informative content consistently.

2. Audience Research: Identify your target audience's interests, preferences, and pain points. Understand who they are, what they care about, and what type of content they are looking for.

3. Competitive Analysis: Examine existing podcasts in your chosen niche. Identify gaps in content that you can fill or ways you can differentiate your podcast.

Choosing a Podcast Format

Podcasts come in various formats, each with its own set of advantages and challenges. Consider the following popular formats:

1. Solo Shows: One host speaks directly to the audience. Ideal for personal storytelling, expert advice, or niche topics.

2.Co-Hosted Shows: Two or more hosts engage in discussions. This format offers dynamic conversations and diverse perspectives.

3. Interview-Based Shows: The host interviews different guests in each episode. This format brings in expert insights and broadens the show's appeal.

4. Panel Discussions: Multiple guests discuss a topic with the host. It provides a range of viewpoints but requires careful moderation.

5. Narrative Storytelling: Episodes tell a story over multiple parts, often with a mix of interviews, narration, and sound design. Suitable for true crime, history, or fictional content.

Creating a Podcast Blueprint

A podcast blueprint is a strategic plan that outlines your podcast's goals, structure, and content. It includes:

1. Goals: Define what you aim to achieve with your podcast (e.g., educate, entertain, inspire, build a community).

2. Target Audience: Describe your ideal listeners, their interests, and how your podcast will meet their needs.

3. Format and Frequency: Decide on your podcast format and how often you will release episodes (weekly, biweekly, monthly).

4. Episode Structure: Outline the typical structure of your episodes, including segments, length, and key elements (intros, outros, ads).

5. Content Calendar: Plan your episodes in advance, including topics, guest appearances, and release dates. This

helps maintain consistency and ensures you always have content ready.

Naming Your Podcast

Your podcast's name is a critical part of your brand identity. It should be:

1. Descriptive: Clearly indicate what your podcast is about.

2. Memorable: Easy to remember and pronounce.

3. Unique: Distinctive enough to stand out from other podcasts.

4. SEO-Friendly: Include keywords that potential listeners might search for.

Steps to naming your podcast:

1. Brainstorm: List potential names that reflect your podcast's theme and tone.

2. Research: Check for name availability on podcast directories, social media platforms, and as a domain name for a website.

3. Get Feedback: Share your top choices with friends, family, or your target audience for their input.

4. Finalize: Choose the name that best represents your podcast and resonates with your audience.

By thoroughly planning your podcast, defining your niche and audience, choosing the right format, creating a detailed blueprint, and selecting an effective name, you set a strong foundation for a successful podcast.

3

Essential Podcasting Equipment

Essential Podcasting Equipment

Microphones: Types and Recommendations

A good microphone is crucial for producing high-quality audio. Here are the main types of microphones to consider:

1. Dynamic Microphones: Durable and less sensitive to background noise, making them ideal for untreated recording environments.

Recommendations: Shure SM7B, Audio-Technica ATR2100x-USB

2. Condenser Microphones: More sensitive and capable of capturing a wider range of frequencies, best used in controlled environments.

Recommendations: Audio-Technica AT2020, Rode NT1-A

3. USB Microphones: Plug-and-play convenience, combining the microphone and audio interface in one. Suitable for beginners and those looking for simplicity.

Recommendations: Blue Yeti, Samson Q2U

Audio Interfaces and Mixers

An audio interface connects your microphone to your computer and converts analog signals to digital. Mixers provide more advanced audio control, allowing you to adjust levels, add effects, and manage multiple audio sources.

1. Audio Interfaces: Essential for using XLR microphones.

Recommendations: Focusrite Scarlett 2i2, PreSonus AudioBox USB

2. Mixers: Useful for more complex setups, particularly with multiple microphones.

Recommendations: Behringer Xenyx Q802USB, Rodecaster Pro

Headphones

Closed-back headphones are recommended for podcasting as they prevent audio bleed into the microphone and allow for accurate monitoring of your recordings.

Recommendations: Audio-Technica ATH-M50x, Sony MDR-7506

Recording and Editing Software

Choose software that matches your technical proficiency and editing needs.

1. Audacity: Free, open-source software suitable for beginners with basic editing needs.

2.Adobe Audition: Professional-grade software with advanced features, ideal for experienced users.

3. GarageBand: Free for Mac users, offering a user-friendly interface for basic to intermediate editing.

Additional Accessories

1. Pop Filter: Reduces plosive sounds (e.g., "p" and "b" sounds).

2. Shock Mount: Isolates the microphone from vibrations and handling noise.

3. Boom Arm or Stand: Holds the microphone in place, allowing for flexible positioning.

4. Acoustic Panels: Help reduce room echo and improve sound quality.

Budget Considerations

It's important to balance quality and cost, especially if you're just starting out. Here's a breakdown of setups for different budgets:

1. Entry-Level Setup (approx. $100-$200):

USB Microphone (e.g., Samson Q2U)

Closed-back headphones (e.g., Audio-Technica ATH-M20x)

Free recording software (e.g., Audacity)

2. Intermediate Setup (approx. $300-$500):

XLR Microphone (e.g., Audio-Technica AT2020)

Audio Interface (e.g., Focusrite Scarlett 2i2)

Mid-range headphones (e.g., Sony MDR-7506)

Pop filter and boom arm

3. Professional Setup (approx. $800+):

High-end XLR Microphone (e.g., Shure SM7B)

Advanced audio interface (e.g., PreSonus Studio 1824c)

Studio-quality headphones (e.g., Beyerdynamic DT 770 Pro)

Acoustic treatment for recording space.

By investing in the right equipment, you ensure that your podcast delivers high-quality audio, which is crucial for attracting and retaining listeners. Start with what you can afford, and upgrade as your podcast grows.

4

Setting Up Your Recording Space

Setting Up Your Recording Space

Choosing the Right Location

The location you choose for recording your podcast plays a significant role in the overall sound quality. Here are key considerations:

1. Quiet Environment: Select a space with minimal background noise. Avoid areas near busy streets, appliances, or other noise sources.

2. Small Room: Smaller rooms typically have less echo compared to larger spaces.

3. Soft Furnishings: Rooms with carpets, curtains, and upholstered furniture help absorb sound and reduce echo.

Soundproofing and Acoustic Treatment

Soundproofing and acoustic treatment are two different but complementary aspects of improving your recording space.

1. Soundproofing: Prevents external noises from entering your recording space. This can involve:

Sealing Gaps: Use weather stripping on doors and windows to seal gaps.

Adding Mass: Increase the density of walls, doors, and windows with materials like mass-loaded vinyl or soundproof curtains.

2. Acoustic Treatment: Enhances the sound quality within your room by controlling reflections, echo, and reverberation. Key components include:

Acoustic Panels: Foam or fiberglass panels that absorb mid to high frequencies, reducing echo.

Bass Traps: Placed in corners to absorb low frequencies, which can cause muddy sound.

Diffusers: Scatters sound waves to avoid a harsh, flat-sounding room.

Setting Up Your Equipment

Proper equipment setup is essential for achieving the best possible sound quality and ensuring a comfortable recording experience.

1. Microphone Placement: Position your microphone to capture the best sound:

Height and Distance: Place the microphone at mouth level and about 6-12 inches away from your mouth. Use a pop filter to minimize plosive sounds.

Angle: Tilt the microphone slightly to avoid direct breath hits.

2. Using a Boom Arm or Stand: Secure your microphone on a boom arm or stand for stability and adjustability. This setup allows you to position the microphone optimally without handling noise.

3. Monitoring: Use closed-back headphones to monitor your recordings in real time. This helps you catch and correct issues like background noise or clipping.

4. Cabling: Keep your cables organized and out of the way to prevent tripping and accidental disconnections. Use cable ties or clips to manage them neatly.

Pre-Recording Checklist

Before you start recording, run through this checklist to ensure everything is set up correctly:

1. Test Equipment: Check that your microphone, headphones, and audio interface are working properly.

2. Audio Levels: Set your recording levels to avoid clipping. Aim for peaks around -6 dB.

3. Quiet Environment: Ensure your recording space is free from background noise. Inform others in your household or workspace to minimize interruptions.

4. Prepare Content: Have your script, notes, or outline ready. Ensure any guests or co-hosts are prepared and briefed.

By carefully choosing and setting up your recording space, you can significantly improve the quality of your podcast recordings, creating a professional and pleasant listening experience for your audience.

5

Recording Your Podcast

Recording Your Podcast

Pre-Recording Checklist

Before you start recording, it's essential to ensure that everything is set up correctly. Here's a pre-recording checklist to help you:

1. Test Equipment: Ensure your microphone, audio interface, headphones, and recording software are working properly.

2. Check Audio Levels: Set your recording levels to avoid clipping. Aim for peaks around -6 dB to -3 dB.

3. Environment Check: Make sure your recording space is quiet and free from interruptions. Close windows and doors, and inform others about your recording session.

4. Prepare Content: Have your script, notes, or episode outline ready. Make sure any guests or co-hosts are prepared and briefed.

5. Hydration and Vocal Warm-Up: Stay hydrated and do a quick vocal warm-up to ensure your voice is in good condition.

Best Practices for Recording Quality Audio

Recording high-quality audio is crucial for producing a professional-sounding podcast. Here are some best practices:

1. Microphone Technique: Maintain a consistent distance (6-12 inches) from the microphone and speak directly into it. Use a pop filter to minimize plosive sounds.

2. Room Acoustics: Record in a treated room to reduce echo and background noise. Use acoustic panels, bass traps, and diffusers if necessary.

3. Monitor While Recording: Use headphones to monitor your audio in real-time. This helps you catch issues like background noise, clipping, or microphone placement problems.

4. Record in High Quality: Use a high-quality audio format such as WAV or AIFF for recording. Avoid compressed formats like MP3 for the initial recording.

5. Backup Recordings: Record a backup track if possible. Use a separate device or software to ensure you don't lose your recording due to technical issues.

Conducting Interviews and Co-Host Dynamics

Interviews and co-hosted shows add variety and depth to your podcast. Here are some tips for managing these formats:

1. Prepare Questions: Research your guest and prepare a list of questions or topics. This helps keep the conversation flowing and ensures you cover all important points.

2. Create a Comfortable Environment: Make your guest feel at ease by explaining the recording process and offering a glass of water. A relaxed guest will give a better interview.

3. Active Listening: Pay attention to your guest's responses and ask follow-up questions. This creates a natural and engaging conversation.

4. Co-Host Coordination: If you have a co-host, establish clear communication and roles. Decide who will lead different segments and how to handle transitions.

5. Avoid Talking Over Each Other: Ensure that only one person speaks at a time. This makes editing easier and creates a better listening experience.

Remote Recording Solutions

Recording with remote guests or co-hosts requires additional considerations to ensure good audio quality:

1. Choose the Right Platform: Use reliable remote recording tools like Zencastr, Riverside.fm, or SquadCast. These platforms offer high-quality audio recording and separate tracks for each participant.

2. Internet Connection: Ensure all participants have a stable and fast internet connection. Wired connections are preferable to Wi-Fi for stability.

3. Use Headphones: All participants should use headphones to prevent audio bleed and echo.

4. Local Recording Backup: If possible, ask your guest to record their audio locally using their smartphone or computer. This can serve as a backup in case of internet issues.

5. Pre-Recording Test: Conduct a test call to check audio levels, internet connection, and platform familiarity. This helps identify and resolve potential issues before the actual recording.

By following these guidelines, you can ensure that your podcast recordings are high quality and professional, whether you're recording solo, with a co-host, or with remote guests.

6

Editing Your Podcast

Editing Your Podcast

Choosing Editing Software

Selecting the right editing software is crucial for producing high-quality podcasts. Here are some popular options:

1. Audacity: A free, open-source editor suitable for beginners. It offers a range of features for basic editing needs.

2. Adobe Audition: A professional-grade editor with advanced features, ideal for experienced users looking for comprehensive editing tools.

3. GarageBand: Free for Mac users, offering a user-friendly interface for basic to intermediate editing.

4. Reaper: An affordable, highly customizable editor with a robust set of features, suitable for both beginners and professionals.

Basic Editing Techniques

Understanding basic editing techniques will help you produce a polished podcast. Key techniques include:

1. Cutting and Trimming: Remove unnecessary parts, such as long pauses, mistakes, or tangents, to keep your podcast concise and engaging.

2. Noise Reduction: Use noise reduction tools to eliminate background noise and improve audio clarity.

3. Equalization (EQ): Adjust the balance of frequencies to enhance the overall sound quality. For example, reduce low frequencies to minimize rumble and boost mid to high frequencies for clarity.

4. Compression: Apply compression to even out the volume levels, ensuring a consistent listening experience.

5. Normalization: Normalize the audio to ensure the overall volume level is appropriate and consistent across episodes.

Advanced Editing Techniques

For more polished and professional-sounding podcasts, consider these advanced techniques:

1. Multitrack Editing: Use multitrack editing to manage different audio sources (e.g., host, guest, music, sound effects) separately, allowing for more precise control.

2. De-essing: Reduce harsh "s" sounds using a de-esser tool to create a smoother listening experience.

3. Audio Restoration: Use tools to repair audio issues like clicks, pops, and distortion.

4. Creative Effects: Add creative effects, such as reverb or delay, to enhance storytelling or create a specific atmosphere.

Adding Music and Sound Effects

Music and sound effects can enhance your podcast and make it more engaging. Here's how to use them effectively:

1. Intro and Outro Music: Choose music that reflects the tone of your podcast. Use it consistently for your intro and outro to create a recognizable brand.

2. Background Music: Use background music sparingly to enhance certain segments without overwhelming the dialogue. Lower the volume so it doesn't compete with the speech.

3. Sound Effects: Add sound effects to emphasize key points, transitions, or storytelling elements. Ensure they are relevant and not distracting.

4.Royalty-Free Sources: Use royalty-free music and sound effects from sources like Incompetech, Free Music Archive, and SoundBible to avoid copyright issues.

Editing for Pacing and Flow

Editing for pacing and flow ensures your podcast is engaging and easy to follow:

1. Smooth Transitions: Use crossfades to create smooth transitions between segments and avoid abrupt cuts.

2. Segment Breaks: Insert brief music or sound effects between segments to signal transitions and maintain listener interest.

3. Maintain Natural Speech: Edit in a way that preserves the natural rhythm and flow of conversation. Avoid making cuts that sound jarring or unnatural.

4. Consistent Length: Aim for a consistent episode length to meet listener expectations. If your podcast varies in length, clearly communicate this to your audience.

#Finalizing and Exporting Your Episode

Once editing is complete, follow these steps to finalize and export your episode:

1. **Listen Through**: Do a final listen-through to catch any remaining issues or errors.
    2. **Metadata**: Add metadata, including episode title, description, artwork, and tags. This information helps listeners find and identify your episodes.

3. **Export Settings**: Export your episode in a high-quality format. Common settings include:
   - **Format**: MP3 or AAC
   - **Bitrate**: 128 kbps to 192 kbps for a balance between quality and file size
   - **Sample Rate**: 44.1 kHz
4. **Backup**: Save a backup copy of your raw and edited files for future reference or re-editing.

By mastering these editing techniques and tools, you can produce professional-quality podcast episodes that captivate and engage your audience.

7

Publishing and Distributing Your Podcast

Publishing and Distributing Your Podcast

Choosing a Podcast Hosting Platform

A podcast hosting platform is essential for storing your audio files and generating an RSS feed, which is used to distribute your podcast to various directories. When selecting a hosting platform, consider the following factors:

Storage and Bandwidth: Ensure the platform offers sufficient storage and bandwidth for your needs.

1. Ease of Use: Look for an intuitive interface that makes uploading and managing episodes simple.
2. Analytics: Choose a platform that provides detailed analytics to track your podcast's performance.

3. Monetization Options: Consider platforms that offer monetization features such as sponsorships, subscriptions, or donations.
4. Customer Support: Reliable customer support can be crucial, especially if you encounter technical issues.

Popular Podcast Hosting Platforms:

Buzzsprout: User-friendly with good analytics and various pricing plans.

Libsyn: One of the oldest and most reliable platforms, with robust features and extensive analytics.

Podbean: Offers unlimited storage and bandwidth, plus monetization options.

Anchor: Free hosting with easy-to-use features, now part of Spotify.

Transistor: Ideal for businesses and networks with multiple shows, offering excellent analytics and distribution.

Submitting Your Podcast to Directories

To reach a wider audience, submit your podcast to major directories. Here are the steps to submit your podcast to the most popular ones:

1. Apple Podcasts:

Create an Apple ID if you don't have one.

Log in to Apple Podcasts Connect.

Validate your RSS feed and submit your podcast for approval.

2. Spotify:

Log in to Spotify for Podcasters.

Submit your RSS feed and fill out the required details.

Wait for approval, which usually takes a few days.

3. Google Podcasts:

Log in to Google Podcasts Manager.

Submit your RSS feed and verify ownership.

Google will index your podcast, making it available in their directory.

4. Stitcher:

Sign up for a Stitcher account and log in.

Submit your RSS feed and fill out the necessary information.

Stitcher will review and approve your submission.

5. Other Directories:

Submit to additional directories like TuneIn, iHeartRadio, Overcast, Pocket Casts, and Castbox by following their specific submission processes.

Optimizing Your Podcast Metadata

Metadata is crucial for helping potential listeners find and understand your podcast. Ensure your metadata is clear, accurate, and engaging:

1. Title: Choose a descriptive and memorable title that reflects the content of your podcast.
2. Description: Write a compelling description that outlines what your podcast is about and what listeners can expect.
3. Episode Titles: Use descriptive episode titles that include keywords related to the content.
4. Artwork: Create eye-catching artwork that meets the directory specifications (usually 1400x1400 to 3000x3000 pixels).
5. Tags and Categories: Use relevant tags and categories to help listeners find your podcast through searches and recommendations.

Promoting Your Podcast

Promotion is key to growing your podcast audience. Here are some effective strategies:

1. Social Media: Share your episodes on social media platforms like Twitter, Facebook, Instagram, and LinkedIn. Use engaging visuals and hashtags to reach a broader audience.
2. Website and Blog: Create a website or blog for your podcast. Write blog posts related to your episodes and embed the audio player.

3. Email Newsletter: Build an email list and send regular updates to your subscribers about new episodes, behind-the-scenes content, and special announcements.
4. Guest Appearances: Appear as a guest on other podcasts to reach new audiences and build credibility.
5. Collaborations: Partner with other podcasters or influencers in your niche for cross-promotion.
6. Paid Advertising: Consider using paid ads on social media, podcast directories, or search engines to boost visibility.

Tracking and Analyzing Your Podcast Performance

Regularly tracking and analyzing your podcast's performance helps you understand your audience and improve your content. Focus on these key metrics:

1. Downloads and Plays: Track the number of downloads and plays to gauge your podcast's reach.
2. Listeners: Monitor the number of unique listeners to understand your audience size.
3. Geographic Data: Analyze where your listeners are located to tailor your content and marketing efforts.

4. Engagement: Look at listener retention rates and average listening duration to see how engaging your episodes are.
5. Episode Performance: Compare the performance of different episodes to identify popular topics and formats.

By choosing the right hosting platform, submitting to directories, optimizing metadata, promoting effectively, and tracking performance, you can successfully publish and distribute your podcast to reach a wide audience and achieve your goals.

8

Marketing and Growing Your Podcast

Marketing and Growing Your Podcast

Building Your Podcast Brand

Creating a strong brand is essential for standing out in the crowded podcasting space. Here's how to build your podcast brand:

1. Define Your Unique Selling Proposition (USP): Identify what makes your podcast unique. This could be your perspective, expertise, style, or the specific niche you cover.

2. Consistent Visual Identity: Develop a consistent visual identity, including your logo, color scheme, and typography. Use these elements across all your platforms to create a cohesive brand image.

3. Voice and Tone: Establish a consistent voice and tone that reflects your podcast's personality. Whether formal, casual, humorous, or inspirational, consistency helps build listener loyalty.

4. Brand Story: Craft a compelling brand story that explains your podcast's mission, vision, and values. Share this story on your website and social media profiles.

Leveraging Social Media

Social media is a powerful tool for promoting your podcast and engaging with your audience. Here are some strategies:

1. Choose the Right Platforms: Focus on the social media platforms where your target audience is most active. Popular choices include Twitter, Instagram, Facebook, and LinkedIn.

2. Engaging Content: Share a variety of content, such as episode teasers, behind-the-scenes photos, guest highlights, quotes, and polls. Use visuals and videos to capture attention.

3. Hashtags: Use relevant hashtags to increase the discoverability of your posts. Create a unique hashtag for your podcast to build a community around your brand.

4. Interact with Your Audience: Respond to comments, messages, and mentions. Engage in conversations and show appreciation for your listeners' support.

5. Collaborations: Partner with influencers, other podcasters, or brands in your niche for cross-promotion and to reach a broader audience.

Utilizing Email Marketing

Email marketing is an effective way to build a loyal audience and keep them informed about your podcast. Here's how to use it effectively:

1. Build an Email List: Encourage your listeners to subscribe to your email list by offering incentives like exclusive content, episode previews, or giveaways.

2. Regular Newsletters: Send regular newsletters with updates on new episodes, behind-the-scenes content, upcoming guests, and special announcements.

3. Personalized Content: Segment your email list based on listener interests and behaviors to send personalized and relevant content.

4. Call to Action (CTA): Include clear CTAs in your emails, such as asking listeners to share episodes, leave reviews, or follow you on social media.

Networking and Collaborations

Networking and collaborations can help you grow your podcast audience and build credibility. Here are some strategies:

1. Guest Appearances: Appear as a guest on other podcasts in your niche to reach new audiences and share your expertise.

2. Guest Hosts: Invite guest hosts to your podcast to provide fresh perspectives and attract their followers to your show.

3. Podcast Networks: Join podcast networks or communities where you can collaborate with other podcasters, share resources, and cross-promote episodes.

4. Industry Events: Attend industry events, webinars, and conferences to connect with other podcasters, potential guests, and industry professionals.

Encouraging Listener Engagement

Engaging with your listeners helps build a loyal community around your podcast. Here are some ways to encourage listener engagement:

1. Listener Questions and Feedback: Encourage listeners to submit questions, feedback, and topic suggestions. Address these in your episodes to make them feel involved.

2. Interactive Content: Create interactive content such as polls, Q&A sessions, and live streams to engage with your audience in real time.

3. Listener Contests and Giveaways: Run contests and giveaways to incentivize listeners to participate and share your podcast.

4. Community Building: Create a dedicated community space, such as a Facebook group or Discord server, where listeners can connect with you and each other.

Measuring and Analyzing Growth

Regularly measuring and analyzing your podcast's growth helps you understand what's working and where you can improve. Focus on these key metrics:

1. Download Trends: Monitor download trends over time to see if your audience is growing.

2. Listener Demographics: Analyze demographic data to understand who your listeners are and tailor your content accordingly.

3. Engagement Metrics: Track metrics such as social media interactions, email open rates, and website traffic to gauge listener engagement.

4. Listener Feedback: Collect and analyze listener feedback to understand what your audience likes and dislikes about your podcast.

5. Monetization Metrics: If you're monetizing your podcast, track metrics like ad revenue, sponsorship deals, and listener donations to measure financial growth.

By implementing these marketing and growth strategies, you can increase your podcast's visibility, attract new listeners, and build a loyal community around your show.

9

Monetizing Your Podcast

Monetizing Your Podcast

Understanding Podcast Monetization

Monetizing your podcast involves generating revenue from your content. While it may take time to build a large enough audience to attract monetization opportunities, understanding the various methods can help you plan and execute your strategy effectively.

Sponsorships and Advertising

One of the most common ways to monetize a podcast is through sponsorships and advertising. Here's how to get started:

1. Identify Potential Sponsors: Look for brands and businesses that align with your podcast's niche and audience. These could be companies your listeners already use or would benefit from.

2. Create a Media Kit: Develop a media kit that includes information about your podcast, audience demographics, download statistics, and sponsorship options. This helps potential sponsors understand the value you offer.

3. Ad Formats: Familiarize yourself with different ad formats:

Pre-Roll Ads: Ads placed at the beginning of the episode.

Mid-Roll Ads: Ads inserted in the middle of the episode.

Post-Roll Ads: Ads placed at the end of the episode.

4. Pricing: Set your ad rates based on your download numbers. Common pricing models include:

Cost Per Mille (CPM): Charges per thousand downloads (e.g., $20 CPM means $20 per 1,000 downloads).

Cost Per Acquisition (CPA): Charges based on the number of conversions (e.g., sales or sign-ups).

5. Ad Integration: Integrate ads seamlessly into your podcast to maintain a positive listener experience. Host-read ads are often more engaging and effective.

Listener Donations and Crowdfunding

Engaging your audience directly for financial support can be an effective way to monetize your podcast. Here are some options:

1. Patreon: A membership platform where listeners can support you with monthly contributions in exchange for exclusive content, early access, and other perks.

2. Buy Me a Coffee: A simple way for listeners to make one-time donations.

3. Crowdfunding Campaigns: Platforms like Kickstarter or Indiegogo allow you to run campaigns to fund specific projects or seasons of your podcast.

Merchandise

Selling merchandise can both monetize your podcast and strengthen your brand. Consider these steps:

1. Create Branded Merchandise: Design items like T-shirts, mugs, stickers, and more with your podcast's logo or catchphrases.

2. Set Up an Online Store: Use platforms like Shopify, Teespring, or Printful to set up an online store.

3. Promote Your Merchandise: Regularly mention your merchandise in episodes and promote it on your social media channels and website.

Premium Content

Offering premium content is another effective way to monetize your podcast. Here's how to do it:

1. Bonus Episodes: Provide extra episodes or extended versions of regular episodes exclusively for paying subscribers.

2. Early Access: Give paying subscribers early access to new episodes.

3. Ad-Free Episodes: Offer ad-free versions of your episodes to subscribers.

4. Exclusive Content: Create content exclusively for subscribers, such as interviews, behind-the-scenes content, or special series.

Affiliate Marketing

Affiliate marketing involves promoting products or services and earning a commission for any sales made through your referral links. Here's how to get started:

1. Join Affiliate Programs: Sign up for affiliate programs that offer products or services relevant to your audience. Examples include Amazon Associates, ShareASale, and CJ Affiliate.

2. Promote Products: Mention and recommend affiliate products naturally within your episodes and provide links in your show notes.

3. Track Performance: Use tracking tools to monitor clicks and conversions from your affiliate links to optimize your strategy.

Offering Services

Leverage your expertise to offer services related to your podcast's niche. Here are some ideas:

1. Consulting or Coaching: Offer one-on-one consulting or coaching sessions in your area of expertise.

2. Workshops and Webinars: Host workshops, webinars, or online courses for your audience.

3. Freelance Services: Offer freelance services like writing, editing, or design, depending on your skills and experience.

Licensing and Syndication

If your podcast content is valuable and high-quality, consider licensing it to other platforms or syndicating it to reach a broader audience. Here's how:

1. Licensing: License your content to other media outlets, websites, or platforms that may want to feature your episodes.

2. Syndication: Syndicate your podcast to radio stations, other podcasts, or platforms looking for content in your niche.

Analyzing and Optimizing Revenue Streams

Regularly analyze and optimize your monetization strategies to maximize revenue:

1. Track Performance: Use analytics to track the performance of your monetization efforts. Monitor metrics like ad revenue, listener donations, merchandise sales, and affiliate conversions.

2. Gather Feedback: Collect feedback from your audience to understand what monetization methods they prefer and are willing to support.

3. Experiment: Don't be afraid to try new monetization methods and strategies. Experiment with different types of content, ad formats, and products to see what works best.

4. Adjust Pricing: Adjust your pricing models based on performance data and market trends. Ensure your pricing reflects the value you provide.

By exploring and implementing these monetization strategies, you can generate revenue from your podcast and build a sustainable, profitable venture.

10

Measuring Success and Continuous Improvement

Measuring Success and Continuous Improvement

Key Metrics to Track

To measure the success of your podcast, track a variety of metrics that provide insights into your audience's behavior and your content's performance. Here are the key metrics to consider:

1. Downloads and Streams: Track the total number of downloads and streams for each episode. This is a primary indicator of your podcast's reach and popularity.

2.Unique Listeners: Monitor the number of unique listeners to understand how many individual people are tuning in to your podcast.

3. Subscriber Growth: Measure the growth of your subscriber base over time. This helps you gauge the retention and attraction of new listeners.

4. Listener Demographics: Analyze demographic data (age, gender, location) to better understand your audience and tailor your content accordingly.

5. Engagement Metrics: Look at metrics like average listening duration, listener retention rates, and completion rates to see how engaging your content is.

6. Social Media Metrics: Track likes, shares, comments, and follower growth on your social media platforms to measure audience engagement and reach.

7. Website Traffic: If you have a website, monitor traffic, page views, and user behavior to see how listeners interact with your online presence.

8. Feedback and Reviews: Collect and analyze listener feedback, reviews, and ratings on podcast directories and social media.

Analyzing Your Data

Regularly analyzing your data helps you make informed decisions to improve your podcast. Here's how to approach it:

1. Identify Trends: Look for patterns and trends in your metrics. For example, notice if certain topics, formats, or guests consistently perform better.

2. Compare Episodes: Compare the performance of different episodes to identify what works and what doesn't. Use this information to refine your content strategy.

3. Audience Insights: Use demographic and engagement data to gain insights into your audience's preferences and behavior. Tailor your content and marketing efforts to better meet their needs.

4. Feedback Analysis: Pay attention to listener feedback and reviews. Identify common themes in the feedback and use them to improve your podcast.

Setting Goals

Setting clear, measurable goals is essential for continuous improvement. Here are some examples of podcasting goals:

1. Audience Growth: Aim to increase your total number of listeners or subscribers by a certain percentage within a specific timeframe.

2. Engagement: Set goals for improving listener engagement metrics, such as average listening duration or social media interactions.

3. Content Quality: Focus on enhancing the quality of your content based on listener feedback and performance data.

4. Monetization: Establish revenue targets from sponsorships, merchandise sales, or listener donations.

5. Production Efficiency: Aim to streamline your production process to reduce the time and effort required to produce each episode.

Strategies for Continuous Improvement

Continuous improvement involves regularly refining your podcast based on data, feedback, and industry trends. Here are some strategies:

1. Content Experimentation: Try different formats, topics, and styles to see what resonates best with your audience. Experiment with solo episodes, interviews, panels, and narrative storytelling.

2. Technical Quality: Invest in better equipment and software to improve the technical quality of your podcast. This includes microphones, audio interfaces, recording software, and editing tools.

3. Professional Development: Continuously learn and improve your podcasting skills. Attend workshops, webinars, and conferences, or take online courses on podcasting, audio editing, marketing, and other relevant topics.

4. Guest Quality: Invite high-quality guests who can provide valuable insights and attract new listeners. Research and reach out to industry experts, influencers, and thought leaders.

5. Audience Engagement: Enhance audience engagement by responding to comments, messages, and reviews. Foster a sense of community through social media interactions, live Q&A sessions, and listener shout-outs.

6. Marketing and Promotion: Regularly review and refine your marketing and promotion strategies. Experiment with new tactics, such as collaborations, paid advertising, or content syndication.

Keeping Up with Industry Trends

Staying informed about industry trends helps you stay competitive and innovative. Here's how to keep up with podcasting trends:

1. Follow Industry News: Subscribe to podcasting blogs, newsletters, and publications to stay updated on the latest news, trends, and best practices.

2. Join Podcasting Communities: Participate in podcasting forums, social media groups, and online communities to connect with other podcasters and share insights.

3. Attend Conferences and Events: Attend podcasting conferences, workshops, and webinars to learn from industry experts and network with other podcasters.

4. Listen to Podcasts: Regularly listen to other podcasts, especially those in your niche, to gain inspiration and understand what's working in the industry.

Adapting to Changes

The podcasting landscape is constantly evolving, and it's important to be adaptable. Here are some tips for staying flexible:

1. Embrace New Technologies: Stay open to adopting new technologies and tools that can enhance your podcasting process and improve the listener experience.

2. Respond to Feedback: Be willing to make changes based on listener feedback and performance data. Regularly solicit feedback and show your audience that you value their input.

3. Stay Agile: Be prepared to pivot your content strategy, marketing approach, or monetization methods if you notice they're not yielding the desired results.

By regularly measuring success, setting clear goals, continuously improving, keeping up with industry trends, and being adaptable, you can ensure the long-term growth and success of your podcast.

11

Legal and Ethical Considerations

Legal and Ethical Considerations

Understanding Copyright and Intellectual Property

Navigating copyright and intellectual property laws is essential for any podcaster to avoid legal issues. Here are some key points to consider:

1. Using Music: Always ensure you have the right to use any music in your podcast. This typically means obtaining a license or using royalty-free music. Platforms like Creative Commons, Incompetech, and Free Music Archive offer music that can be used legally.

2. Third-Party Content: If you include any third-party content (e.g., audio clips, quotes, articles), make sure you have the right to use it. This might involve getting permission from

the content owner or ensuring it falls under fair use, which is often complex and requires careful consideration.

3. Original Content: Protect your own content by understanding your intellectual property rights. You automatically own the copyright to your original content, but you might consider registering it for additional protection.

Permissions and Releases

Obtaining permissions and releases is crucial when using content that involves other people. Here's how to handle this:

1. Guest Releases: Have your guests sign a release form that grants you the right to use their voice and likeness in your podcast. This form should cover all potential uses, including marketing and promotional materials.

2. Location Releases: If you record in a location that is not your own, ensure you have permission to do so. Some public or private spaces may require location releases.

3. Content Releases: For any third-party content, secure written permission to use it. This includes audio clips, music, and quotes.

Ethical Considerations

Maintaining high ethical standards is essential for building trust with your audience and guests. Here are some guidelines:

1. Transparency: Be transparent about any sponsorships, ads, or affiliate relationships. Disclose these relationships clearly to your audience.

2. Fact-Checking: Ensure the accuracy of the information you present. Fact-check your content to maintain credibility and avoid spreading misinformation.

3. Respecting Privacy: Respect the privacy of your guests and audience. Do not share personal information without explicit consent.

4. Balanced Content: Strive to present balanced and fair content, especially on controversial topics. Avoid sensationalism and ensure your content is respectful and considerate of different viewpoints.

Dealing with Defamation and Libel

Avoiding defamation and libel is crucial to protecting yourself from legal action. Here's how to stay on the right side of the law:

1. Defamation and Libel: Defamation involves making false statements that harm someone's reputation. Libel is written defamation, while slander is spoken defamation.

2. Truth and Opinion: Ensure that any statements you make about individuals or entities are true and can be substantiated. Clearly differentiate between factual statements and opinions.

3. Avoiding Harm: Avoid making statements that could be perceived as harmful or damaging to someone's reputation. If in doubt, consult a legal professional.

Privacy Laws and Regulations

Understanding and complying with privacy laws and regulations is essential, especially if you collect any personal information from your listeners. Key points include:

1. Data Protection: If you collect personal data (e.g., email addresses for a newsletter), ensure you comply with data protection laws like the General Data Protection Regulation

(GDPR) in the EU or the California Consumer Privacy Act (CCPA) in the US.

2. Consent: Obtain explicit consent from your listeners before collecting and using their personal data. Provide clear information about how their data will be used.

3. Security: Implement measures to protect the data you collect from unauthorized access or breaches.

Trademark Issues

Trademarks protect brand names, logos, and other identifiers. Here's what you need to know:

1. Choosing a Name: Before finalizing your podcast name, conduct a trademark search to ensure it's not already in use. This helps avoid potential legal conflicts.

2. Trademark Registration: Consider registering your podcast name and logo as trademarks to protect your brand identity. This provides legal protection against unauthorized use.

3. Respecting Others' Trademarks: Avoid using trademarks owned by others without permission. This includes names, logos, and any distinctive branding elements.

Contracts and Agreements

Contracts and agreements are important for formalizing relationships and protecting your interests. Here are some common agreements you might encounter:

1. Guest Agreements: Use guest release forms to clarify the terms of their participation and your right to use their contributions.

2. Sponsorship Agreements: Create detailed agreements with sponsors that outline the terms of the sponsorship, including deliverables, payment terms, and duration.

3. Co-Host Agreements: If you have co-hosts, establish clear agreements about roles, responsibilities, and revenue sharing to avoid misunderstandings.

Staying Informed and Seeking Legal Advice

Laws and regulations can be complex and vary by jurisdiction. It's important to stay informed and seek professional advice when needed:

1. Legal Resources: Use resources like podcasts, blogs, and webinars from legal professionals to stay updated on relevant laws and best practices.

2. Consult a Lawyer: If you have specific legal questions or concerns, consult a lawyer who specializes in intellectual property or media law. They can provide tailored advice and help you navigate complex legal issues.

By understanding and adhering to legal and ethical considerations, you can protect yourself and your podcast, build trust with your audience, and ensure a long-lasting, reputable presence in the podcasting world.

12

Case Studies and Success Stories

Case Studies and Success Stories

Case Study 1: "Serial" - Transforming True Crime Podcasting

Overview

"Serial," created by Sarah Koenig and Julie Snyder, revolutionized the podcasting world when it debuted in 2014. This investigative journalism podcast, focusing on a true crime story over multiple episodes, quickly became a cultural phenomenon.

Key Strategies for Success

1. Engaging Storytelling: "Serial" captivated listeners with its in-depth, serialized storytelling format. Each episode ended on a cliffhanger, encouraging binge-listening.

2. High Production Quality: The podcast invested heavily in production quality, including sound design, music, and meticulous editing.

3. Multimedia Integration: "Serial" complemented its audio content with an informative website featuring documents, maps, and additional resources, enhancing listener engagement.

4. Audience Interaction: The podcast encouraged audience interaction through social media and email, creating a dedicated community of listeners.

Lessons Learned

The power of compelling storytelling in creating listener loyalty.

The importance of high production values in setting a podcast apart.

The value of integrating multimedia elements to enrich the audience experience.

Case Study 2: "The Joe Rogan Experience" - Building a Podcast Empire

Overview

Joe Rogan's podcast, "The Joe Rogan Experience," launched in 2009, has grown to become one of the most popular and influential podcasts globally, featuring a wide range of guests from various fields.

Key Strategies for Success

1. Diverse Guest Lineup: Rogan's podcast features an eclectic mix of guests, including comedians, scientists, politicians, and celebrities, attracting a diverse audience.

2. Long-Form Content: The long, conversational format allows for deep dives into topics, providing in-depth discussions that engage listeners for hours.

3. Consistency: Rogan consistently releases episodes, creating a reliable schedule that keeps listeners coming back.

4. Platform Expansion: Rogan has expanded his reach by maintaining a strong presence on YouTube and other platforms, in addition to traditional podcast directories.

Lessons Learned

Diversity in guests and topics can broaden audience appeal.

Long-form content can successfully engage listeners if the discussions are compelling.

Consistency is key in building and maintaining an audience.

Expanding to multiple platforms can significantly increase reach and visibility.

Case Study 3: "How I Built This" - Inspiring Entrepreneurial Stories

Overview

NPR's "How I Built This," hosted by Guy Raz, showcases the stories behind successful entrepreneurs and their companies. The podcast has become a go-to source of inspiration for aspiring entrepreneurs.

Key Strategies for Success

1. Inspirational Content: The podcast focuses on success stories and challenges, providing valuable insights and inspiration for listeners.

2. Strong Host Presence: Guy Raz's interviewing style and rapport with guests add depth and personality to the episodes.

3. High-Profile Guests: Featuring well-known entrepreneurs and industry leaders attracts a large audience interested in learning from successful figures.

4. Narrative Style: The podcast uses a narrative style that blends interviews with storytelling, making the content engaging and accessible.

Lessons Learned

Inspirational and educational content can attract a dedicated listener base.

The host's personality and interviewing skills play a crucial role in the podcast's success.

Featuring high-profile guests can significantly boost credibility and audience interest.

A narrative style that combines interviews with storytelling can enhance listener engagement.

Case Study 4: "Stuff You Should Know" - Educating with Entertainment

Overview

"Stuff You Should Know," hosted by Josh Clark and Chuck Bryant, is an educational podcast that explains how things work and explores a wide range of topics. Launched in 2008, it has become one of the most popular podcasts in its genre.

Key Strategies for Success

1. Broad Topic Range: The podcast covers an extensive range of topics, appealing to a wide audience with diverse interests.

2. Entertaining Delivery: The hosts use humor and a conversational tone to make complex topics accessible and enjoyable.

3. Consistency: Regular release of episodes has built a loyal listener base.

4. Listener Engagement: The podcast engages with its audience through social media, listener mail segments, and live shows.

Lessons Learned

Covering a broad range of topics can attract a diverse audience.

Using humor and a conversational tone can make educational content more engaging.

Consistency helps in building and retaining an audience.

Engaging with listeners through multiple channels enhances loyalty and community.

Case Study 5: "My Favorite Murder" Building a Community around Truc Crime

Overview

"My Favorite Murder," hosted by Karen Kilgariff and Georgia Hardstark, blends true crime with comedy. Launched in 2016, it has developed a dedicated fan base known as "Murderinos."

Key Strategies for Success

1. Unique Format: The blend of true crime storytelling with humor sets the podcast apart from other true crime shows.

2. Strong Community: The podcast has cultivated a strong community, with active social media groups and fan events.

3. Merchandising: The podcast monetizes through merchandise, offering products that resonate with their audience.

4. Listener Participation: Incorporating listener-submitted stories and feedback fosters a sense of involvement and loyalty.

Lessons Learned

A unique format can differentiate a podcast in a crowded market.

Building a strong community can enhance listener loyalty and engagement.

Merchandise can be a successful revenue stream if it aligns with the audience's interests.

Encouraging listener participation creates a sense of ownership and connection.

Conclusion: Key Takeaways from Successful Podcasts

These case studies highlight several key strategies and lessons for aspiring podcasters:

1. Storytelling and Content: Compelling storytelling and high-quality content are crucial for engaging listeners.

2. Consistency: Regularly releasing episodes helps build a loyal audience.

3. Audience Engagement: Actively engaging with your audience through social media, feedback, and events fosters community and loyalty.

4. Adaptability: Being open to experimenting with different formats, topics, and platforms can lead to greater success.

5. Monetization: Diversifying revenue streams through sponsorships, merchandise, and premium content can make a podcast financially sustainable.

By learning from these successful podcasts, you can apply their strategies and insights to your own podcasting journey, increasing your chances of building a successful and enduring show.

All Rights Reserved
Olivia Westwood
2024